Victorian Marblehead

Commentary by Gail P. Hercher

Photographs by Michael Hercher

The Sometime Press, Inc.
Marblehead, Massachusetts
1980

Front cover: 25 High Street
Inside covers: 264 Pleasant Street
Back cover: Gut 'n Feathers Club

Library of Congress Catalog Card Number: 80-50011

ISBN 0-936230-24-X

Printed in the United States of America by Wilkscraft Creative Printing, Beverly, Massachusetts 01915.

Published by
The Sometime Press, Inc.
P.O. Box 986, Marblehead, Massachusetts 01945
First printing, 1980.

iv

Contents

Preface vii

Introduction   1

Victorian Buildings in Marblehead   9

    Italianate Style 1840-1880 11
    Gothic Revival and Carpenter Gothic Ornament 15
    Mansard Style 21
    Eastern Stick Style 29
    Queen Anne Style 41
    Eastlake Decoration 53
    Shingle Style 61
    Victorian Gothic Style 71
    Octagon House 79
    19th Century Commercial Brick Buildings 83
    Alpine Chalet 91
    Chateau Style 95
    English Tudor Style 99
    Mission Style 105
    Colonial Revival 109
    The American Castle 113
    Neo Classic Revival 117
    Triple Decker Style 121
    Details 125

For Further Reading 139

About the Authors 141

Preface

Not very long ago people were embarrassed by the decorative exuberance of Victorian architecture and as a result many Victorian structures were 'improved' or otherwise disguised. Fortunately, people now treasure the legacy of the Victorian era, realizing that such richness of detail may never again be possible.

One of the purposes of this book has been to record some of the remaining 19th century buildings in Marblehead, with the hope that these buildings will be as prized and protected as their colonial antecedents. Unfortunately, not every 19th century building in Marblehead could be included in this survey, and of the several hundred Victorian structures in town, only a sampling are featured in this book. Considerable latitude has been taken in choosing the buildings to be pictured; some are included for aesthetic reasons and some for historic reasons. The several examples of early 20th century architecture shown are particularly interesting as remnants of the Victorian period.

It is hoped that the essay that introduces the photographs, although not a thorough treatise, will place the Marblehead buildings in the context of their time and place, and that the style descriptions will help to differentiate the many Victorian building types. With the aid of a map, the reader should be able to find the buildings, although it should be kept in mind that, with few exceptions, all are privately owned and their occupants should therefore not be disturbed.

Many sources were consulted for the historical material in this book, but *Marblehead, The Spirit of '76 Lives Here* by Priscilla Lord and Virginia Gamage (Chilton Book Co., 1972), *Boston's North Shore* by Joseph E. Garland (Little, Brown & Co., 1978), and *The History and Traditions of Marblehead* by Samuel Roads (Houghton Mifflin Co., 1880), are particularly recommended to anyone interested in the general history of Marblehead. For books on architectural taste and history, those suggested in 'For Further Reading' should be found germane.

The emphasis of this book is on the beauty of 19th century architecture and although Marblehead is not another Newport — her architecture is not as grand — Marblehead does have many fine examples of 19th century architecture that can be justifiably cherished.

GPH
Marblehead, 1980

Introduction

Most 19th century American architectural styles were revivals of former styles, or even revivals of revivals, and it is this architecture that we have come to call 'Victorian.'

Following the tradition in which the name of the British monarch was used to characterize style and taste during his or her reign (Edwardian, Georgian, etc.), the word 'Victorian' refers to a period of time, namely, the years of Queen Victoria's reign (1837-1901), although some historians extend the period to the outbreak of the First World War. 'Victorian,' then, applies to all the styles that evolved while the Queen was alive — Gothic Revival, Victorian Gothic, Italianate, Second Empire, Eastern Stick, Shingle, Queen Anne, and so on. While most of the styles had their origins in Europe and appeared on the American scene after a short time lag, a few of the styles were revivals or continuations of earlier indigenous American styles (enthusiasm for which was generated by the 1876 Centennial Celebration); toward the close of the century, a few styles evolved that were uniquely American.

Early in the 19th century, architects and the public at large attached symbolic meaning to the different architectural styles. Roman Revival, the symbol of civic virtue, was considered appropriate for public buildings; Greek Revival, the symbol of liberty, was popular for the homes of democratic citizens across the United States; Egyptian Revival, the symbol of permanence, was used in cemeteries; and the Gothic Revival was deemed especially fitting for ecclesiastical architecture since it represented Christian ideals. By the late 1850's, however, this rather rigid system began to break down and a mixing of the styles became fashionable, and eventually almost obligatory. By the close of the century, motifs from English, French, Italian, Greek, Middle Eastern and Oriental sources all served as inspiration to Victorian designers, sometimes reproduced accurately, but more often combined in new and fantastic ways.

After the Civil War, as America grew in importance and society became more complex, so did her architecture and American homes became larger, more comfortable, and more ornate. It was at this time that gadgets became popular, systems for ventilating, water delivery, lighting and heating became common, and speaking tubes became the rage!

A surprisingly large number of people chose to live in informal, personalized, or even wildly eccentric houses, and although some of these owners may have spent more money on their houses than would seem sane, Americans were enjoying a new and high level of prosperity which may have accounted for their extravagance. During the 19th century the most vital architecture in America was built with 'new' money because the 19th century businessman or industrial magnate was as likely to be as aggressively individualistic in architecture as he was in business.

Victorian house builders consciously set out to design houses that they perceived as beautiful, having grown tired of the severe Classical and Greek Revival modes and, since they believed that decoration was an integral part of beauty, the result was an emphasis on ornament. A great deal of the impetus for this ornament was provided by the development of power driven tools which allowed ornamentation to be easily and inexpensively produced. Throughout the United States local mills issued annual catalogues which offered hundreds of variations of wooden decorative ornaments; millwork items were also custom made to the specifications of builders and architects, many of whom adopted particular millwork combinations as their personal signature detail. Inexpensive millwork, plus the availability of standardized lumber, commercially made paints, brushes, nails, and the relatively new balloon-frame method of construction, increased house building efficiency and at the same time enabled people to have abundant decorative detail at a price they could afford.

Another standardizing factor in house building across the United States in the 19th century was the appearance of the house pattern book, of which Walter's *Two Hundred Designs for Cottages and Villas* (1846), Palliser's *New Cottage Homes* (1887), and Calvert Vaux's *Villas & Cottages* (1863) were among the most popular.

Philosophical books on architecture by Andrew Jackson Downing (1815-1852), a self-trained landscape architect who sought to create what he termed 'suitable' homes for the middle class, were also widely read. According to Downing, since the Georgian, Federalist, and Greek Revival styles were based on pagan (Greek and Roman) ideas, they were unsuitable in the United States and instead, the Gothic style based on Christian forms was more appropriate. Through his books *Cottage Residences* (1843) and especially *The Architecture of Country Houses* (1850), which sold 16,000 copies by the end of the Civil War, Downing became the principal proponent of the Gothic Revival style in America and as such considerably changed the course of American architecture. He is credited by some historians as having provided American architecture with its vertical emphasis and it is due primarily to Downing's influence that the insistence upon symmetry as seen in Georgian, Federal and Greek Revival houses lost ground in favor of asymmetry, irregularity, complexity, and the 'picturesque.'

Downing may have been the most influential author, but others left their mark as well. Orson Squire Fowler's volume on the octagonal mode of building, *A Home For All or the Gravel Wall and the Octagon Mode of Building* (1848), was the inspiration for over one thousand octagonal houses in the United States (including one in Marblehead) and Charles Locke Eastlake's *Hints on Household Taste,* originally published in England in 1868 and reissued seven times in the United States between 1872 and 1883, had tremendous impact on the design taste of Americans. All of these authors eschewed the Greek Revival mode in favor of a more 'picturesque' and functional architecture in which structures were asymmetrically organized, harmoniously placed on the site, and painted in autumnal colors to blend into the landscape. At first Victorian home owners used two contrasting exterior paint colors, one for the house body and one for the trim, but as the century progressed combinations of three, four, or even five colors were popular.

There were three levels of Victorian architecture, the Lower, Middle, and Upper, and although earlier architectural historians have tended to place greater importance on the Upper type of architecture, today an increasingly large number of historians and preservationists are focusing on the Lower and Middle types since it is believed that they more broadly reflect a given time in history.

Lower Victorian architecture occurred outside the architectural mainstream and was designed by the anonymous carpenter-builder, rarely by an architect. Frequently, the carpenter-builder (or developer) bought adjacent lots of land (generally near a transportation line) where a row of houses was built on speculation. Such homes were usually identical in plan except for the minor choices of decoration that were left open to the buyer. It was possible to build a modest three or four room cottage for under 1000 dollars; a typical row house cost between one and four thousand dollars to build depending upon its size and the materials used. In some cases the buyer could borrow money from the builder to buy such property; in urban areas (if he worked for a large company) it was often possible for the buyer to borrow money for a house purchase against his salary.

Middle Victorian architecture was frequently created through a collaboration between the owner (usually a businessman or professional person) and the builder. Working together, the two chose house plans from pattern books, ornament from mill catalogs, and made personalized modifications along the way. Such residences, which often included a stable or coachhouse, typically cost between five and ten thousand dollars to build, since they were larger, sturdier, more embellished, and more unique than the houses built on speculation by carpenter-builders and developers.

Upper Victorian architecture was financed by wealthy owners who could afford to hire trained artist-architects to design their residences. These architects may have glanced at house pattern books, mill catalogs, and the popular books on architecture, but they were most influenced by their professional training, the newly founded professional journals, and trips abroad. Upper Victorian homes required large — sometimes even astronomical — amounts of money to build, but they reflected the optimism, confidence, and prosperity of late 19th century America.

In Marblehead there are few examples of Upper Victorian architecture, but there are many examples of the Lower and Middle types which document the history and economic development of the town.

In the very early days, Marblehead was the province of the Naumkeag Indians, members of the Algonquin tribe who in the summer hunted and farmed the area they called 'Massabequash.' The Naumkeags were friendly to the white settlers who established themselves in 1629 in Massabequash; by 1632 the area was known as Marblehead, owing to the belief that there was plenty of marble stone in the area (there is, in fact, none). The Indians, sadly, were so reduced in number by wars and disease over the years that they seem to have played no significant role in the development of Marblehead.

Up until 1648 Marblehead was part of the adjacent town of Salem and was well known as a fishing village. Beginning in 1636 Salem agreed to grant land to the fishermen, although it was stipulated that such lots could not exceed two acres in size, and that they should be primarily intended as a place for a house, garden, and fish flake, or drying rack. In addition to the grants of land to fishermen, in 1635 two eminent shareholders in the Massachusetts Bay Company — John Humphrey, Esq. and Reverend Hugh Peter — were given large tracts of land abutting one another which included all of what are now the Clifton, Clifton Heights, and Devereux sections of Marblehead.

Because they were fishermen, the first settlers in Marblehead built their houses around Little Harbor so as to be close to their boats. Early travelers to Marblehead observed that the clapboard homes were packed close together and that because of the fish flakes, an unpleasant odor wafted over the settlement. Proper siting for the fish flakes (they needed sun and air), as well as the fact that people wanted to be close to each other for security and warmth, very much determined the location of the houses, and since they were built along already existing Indian trails and early pathways, the result was the labyrinth of streets that remains a charming feature of 'Old Town' to this day.

By 1664 there were 44 Commoners, their families and other people living in Marblehead; by 1700 it is believed that there were about 125 houses. Most of these early dwellings have disappeared, having been replaced by larger houses as their owners became more prosperous.

Between 1700 and 1780 many people moved to Marblehead, attracted by the promise of good fishing and the hope of prosperity. Some people were no doubt also attracted to the town because of its reputation as a haven for individualists and eccentrics.

In 1724 Marblehead was divided into three divisions: Lower and Middle, which were near Little Harbor, and Upper, toward Salem. Few people lived in the Upper Division which was the farmland around present-day Gatchell's Park, but as the area around Little Harbor became congested people moved outward along Pleasant and Washington Streets. (Some people thought Marblehead was getting *too* crowded and in 1734 this group petitioned the General Court for a grant of land in the far north where they proposed to establish a settlement that would be called 'New Marblehead.' The group received the grant of land, but the settlement was not successful and the original proprietors eventually sold their rights. The settlement was later renamed Windham, Maine.)

Mid-18th century found Marblehead in its 'Golden Age of Trade' and every facet of town life reflected the general prosperity. Emerging merchant kings built mansions along the major thoroughfares, such as the Georgian style Jeremiah Lee Mansion on Washington Street which was built in 1768. It is believed that by 1740 there were about 450 houses in Marblehead, and by 1790 there were 690 homes reflecting all levels of affluence.

Because Marbleheaders were actively involved in the War for Independence, the town experienced a subsequent period of economic depression and as a result Marblehead was unable to fully recover her pre-war shipping tonnage; the fishing and shipbuilding industries were also depressed. Total economic recovery was further delayed by the War of 1812 since again there were financial setbacks. Despite the reversals, by using captured and surviving vessels from the wars, fishing continued as the major industry in Marblehead well into the 19th century.

In addition to fishing, however, other businesses and industries grew in Marblehead, especially shoemaking. Marbleheaders had always made their own shoes and boots and although it was done on a part-time basis by women at home and men between fishing trips, in the early 1800's cordwaining, or making shoes, was recognized as a significant part of the economy.

In Marblehead, the 'put-out' system was used in which cut shoe uppers were issued to women from a central shop. After they were sewn, the uppers were returned for cash payment; men then finished the shoes in cordwainer shacks which were often shared by a small group for this purpose. Besides cordwaining, factories for manufacturing hats, candles, tinware, chairs, cabinets, soap, glue, cord, and wheels were also established in Marblehead during the early years of the 19th century and were so successful that by 1837 the income from manufactured goods exceeded that from fishing.

In 1838 the Eastern Railroad Branch from Marblehead to Salem opened and pressure mounted for a direct line to Boston, since it was felt that such railroad service would help business. Spurred by industrial growth, significant property development in 'Mid-town' Marblehead began at about this time. Housing was built for factory workers and 'Bowdenville,' around present-day Bowden Street, sprouted up along the railroad line.

In 1846 a terrible storm at sea resulted in the loss of many Marblehead ships and men. This was perhaps the final blow to fishing as a major industry in Marblehead, for after the storm widows and fatherless children were increasingly forced to rely on cordwaining to get by. Gradually, the influx of factories reduced the importance of the 'put-out' system and it soon vanished altogether; by 1857 five large shoe factories were located in Marblehead and they employed the largest percentage of people of any industry in town.

The Civil War generated a need for shoes which increased business in Marblehead, and even after the War the shoe business continued to boom as

North Shore shoes became known throughout the United States and Europe. Marblehead was particularly well known for making fine children's shoes. During the period of post-Civil War economic optimism, many workers found themselves in a position to build or buy a small home and as a result many Victorian homes in Marblehead date from around this time. Owners of the thriving businesses and factories built stately homes on the main streets such as that at 264 Pleasant Street (now Pleasant Manor) which was built in 1872 by Otis Roberts, a shoe box manufacturer.

The opening of the Swampscott Branch of the Eastern Railroad in 1873, which offered direct service to Boston, helped Marblehead business a great deal, so much so that despite a brief economic recession, the Centennial year found Marbleheaders again in a generally optimistic mood. Everyone hailed the laying of the cornerstone of the new Town Hall (Abbot Hall) in 1876 as the symbol of a bright future.

The optimism was obscured on June 25, 1877, when fire broke out and seventy-two buildings in Marblehead were destroyed, including houses, shoe factories, stores and hotels, the newspaper, the railroad depot, South Church and the central fire station. Ninety families were left homeless and 1500 people were left unemployed by the fire, but citizens banded together to help each other and a business recovery plan was put into effect with the result that Marbleheaders were confident that they would soon prosper again.

But a further blow to Marblehead industry came on Christmas Day, 1888, when fire once again swept through the center of town. This time fifty buildings were destroyed, including a number of shoe factories, and two thousand people were put out of work. There were valiant attempts to encourage industry to stay, but most moved away, thus ending Marblehead's 'Golden Age of Industry.'

The shoe industry continued as an important, but not dominant part of the Marblehead economy through the first quarter of the 20th century, but at the same time a new base for the economy developed, namely, the summer visitor.

Partly because it had become easily accessible by train from Boston, in the years following the Civil War Marblehead was a popular place for day trips and longer summer holidays, and by the 1880's was firmly established as a summer resort. (In 1919 the Board of Trade was pleased to report that the population of Marblehead rose from 7,600 in the winter to 12,000 in the summer!) A number of hotels accommodated the summer visitors who came not only from Boston, Salem, New York, and Philadelphia, but from all over the United States. Guests at hotels like the Rockmere (where Glover Landing is now) and the Nanapashmet (on the Neck) were announced weekly in the newspaper. Dr. Frank Leroy Purdy and family, for example, were reported to have arrived at the Rockmere from Brookline in their $10,000 automobile!

For many summer residents and visitors, Marblehead's fine harbor was the major attraction since it was an ideal base for pleasure sailing and racing. When three yacht clubs — the Eastern, Corinthian, and Pleon — established themselves in Marblehead in the 1880's they served to underline the town's position as the yachting capital of the United States.

Many of the people who came to Marblehead in the summer wanted to build homes for their families where there was no congestion and where they could be assured summer breezes, ocean views, and land. The result was the development of Peach's Point, Naugus Head, the Neck and the Clifton and Devereux sections.

Peach's Point, named after one of the founding settlers of Marblehead, John Peach, was mostly pasture and orchard until 1871, when Francis W. Crowninshield of the Salem shipping family purchased a major portion of it (for $9,500) where he built a summer home. His son expanded the property and slowly the Point was transformed from farmland into a summer colony by the Crowninshields and their friends.

Until the 19th century, very few people were interested in living on Marblehead Neck, an area of about three hundred acres connected to the peninsula of Marblehead by an isthmus. It had been a summer camping ground of the Naumkeags, and was long a popular place for picnics and outings, but at the end of the 18th century there were only a few houses on the Neck.

After the War of 1812, Ephraim Brown purchased a large section of the Neck (paying $6,475 for 130 acres) and by adding to his holdings over the years eventually owned 240 acres. Brown ran a fine farm on the Neck and sent his produce to Boston and New York aboard his own schooners which departed from his private dock (now Pleon pier).

In 1867 a piece of land on the Neck was bought by a group of residents from Nashua, New Hampshire. At Nashua Village, as it was called, tents were put up and makeshift cottages were built for summer use. In addition to these campers, people from Lowell leased land on the Neck where they set up their tents at 'Camp Lowell.'

The beginning of the end of casual camping days on the Neck occurred in 1872 when the Brown heirs sold their land at auction to the Marblehead Great Neck Land Company for $255,000, at which time the property was divided into 250 lots. In 1878, however, the mortgage was foreclosed, and the property reverted to the administrators of the Brown estate. Again the property was divided and sold, and within two years (by 1880) there were 68 elegant homes on the Neck, many of which were built in the fashionable Shingle and Eastern Stick styles which were considered particularly suitable for seaside settings. In the closing years of the 19th century the Neck was an active sub-community of Marblehead with its own post office, meeting hall, store, newspaper, and ferry to the mainland.

The creation of Atlantic Avenue in 1870, which enabled people to reach 'Midtown' and 'Old Town' easily from the Clifton and Devereux sections, contributed to the development of these areas of Marblehead. Not coincidentally, the largest remaining section of the Devereux Land (originally part of Reverend Hugh Peter's grant) was sold at about this time, and except for the open area along Devereux Beach, was divided into house lots. Many of these lots were bought by summer residents who proceeded to build their summer homes there. Most of the land originally granted to John Humphrey, Esq., which was nearer Salem, was not developed until after the First World War.

Victorian architecture in Marblehead mirrors the tastes and fortunes of its citizens. To be sure, many 19th century citizens continued to live quite happily in their 18th century houses, while others 'modernized' their colonial homes with Victorian trim. Those who built new houses, however, regardless of their level of income, rejected the familiar classical styles in favor of the new styles like the Mansard and Gothic Revival. Later in the century Marbleheaders also favored the Queen Anne, Stick and Shingle styles for their homes.

No doubt many fine Victorian buildings in Marblehead were destroyed in the calamitous fires of 1877 and 1888, and many others have been lost through insensitive remodeling and demolition. The interesting and diverse examples of 19th century architecture that have survived, however, testify to the vitality of a time past in which people of all levels of income, background, education, and ambition were able to build houses and live in Marblehead. Now in their second century of use, Victorian houses in Marblehead generously add their charm to the town and provide warm homes for the people who live in them.

Victorian Buildings
in Marblehead

In the pages that follow, the photographs of Victorian buildings in Marblehead have been grouped by architectural style and are preceded by a brief description. Since elements of several styles and periods were frequently combined, Victorian buildings rarely adhere precisely to a particular style description or to the dates assigned to that style. The fact that Victorian buildings so often defy categorization, however, is part of their charm.

10

The Italianate Style, 1840-1880

The Italianate home, in which picturesque and romantic elements were combined to create a peaceful atmosphere, was intended to serve as a retreat from the hectic pace of 19th century life. Inspired by rural Italian architecture, heavy wooden brackets or pendants under the eaves and over doors and windows were the major decorative feature of this style. Also common were towers or cupolas and projecting porches and window bays; the semi-circular arch was also a popular motif. Tall, thin first floor windows, often paired in groups of two or three, and a low-pitched roof were characteristic of Italianate buildings, the majority of which were made of wood.

62 Pleasant Street

Highland Terrace

14

The Gothic Revival Style and Carpenter Gothic Ornament, 1830-1865

Inspired by Andrew Jackson Downing's plea for the 'picturesque' in architecture, the Gothic Revival style became popular for residential, ecclesiastical and civic architecture as a welcome alternative to the previous Greek Revival mode; Carpenter Gothic ornament, so named after the carpenters who designed and made it, decorated countless Gothic Revival homes across the United States before the Civil War.

Expensive Gothic Revival buildings displayed Gothic features such as pointed windows, tracery, irregularity, verticality, and were graced with carved and turned ornament; but for the less expensive Gothic Revival homes of the working class, carpenters substituted sawn, drilled, cut and appliqued ornament. These box-like houses with high-peaked roofs were distinguished by fanciful wooden trim, often referred to as 'gingerbread,' which adorned windows and gables. Some of the most imaginative wooden ornament of this type appeared on the bargeboard or vergeboard, the board covering the projecting end of a house gable. The exteriors of modest cottages were often finished with vertical planks and strips in the board and batten technique.

In Marblehead, very little Carpenter Gothic ornament has survived.

15

16

206 Humphrey Street

9 Village Street

11 Village Street

206 Humphrey Street

71 Green Street

Linden Street

20

The Mansard Style, 1860-1890

Generally believed to have been named after the French architect Francois Mansart (1598-1666), a designer of the Louvre, the Mansard style building was characterized by the pitch of the roof, the silhouette of which on the uppermost story was straight, convex, or concave. Frequently such 'French' roofs were covered with colored slate or tinplates and were capped by iron cresting. Other distinguishing features on the two or three story block-like Mansard building included tall first floor windows, verandas, piazzas, and porches; cornices and classical moldings were emphasized by a dramatic use of texture and colored materials.

The Mansard Style was popular for houses built on speculation (there are several of these on Maverick Street in Marblehead), but it was also used for more expensive homes such as number 264 Pleasant Street, where it was enlarged and topped with an Italianate cupola.

102 Front Street

18 Sewall Street

264 Pleasant Street

31 Prospect Street

93 Rockaway Avenue

1 Jefferson Street

28

The Eastern Stick Style, 1860-1890

Considered a distinctly American phenomenon, the Stick Style house was an attempt to be truthful in wooden construction by revealing the basic structure. 'Picturesque' in the sense that Andrew Jackson Downing used the term, the distinguishing feature of the Stick Style was the decorative use of vertical and diagonal 'sticks' (boards) on exterior surfaces, which emphasized the basic form of the building. Along with the counterplay of different textures and patterns of shingles, Stick Style houses were further characterized by large verandas and porches, towers and steeply pitched gables. Stick Style houses were considered particularly appropriate in seaside and vacation settings and were often built up on posts so as to allow air to circulate underneath.

Follett Street

5 Peabody Avenue

West Orchard Street

32

Corinthian Lane

Corinthian Lane

Corinthian Lane

34

Corinthian Lane

5 Peabody Avenue

12 Surf Street

Harvard Street

5 Peabody Avenue

12 Surf Street

38

Clifton Avenue

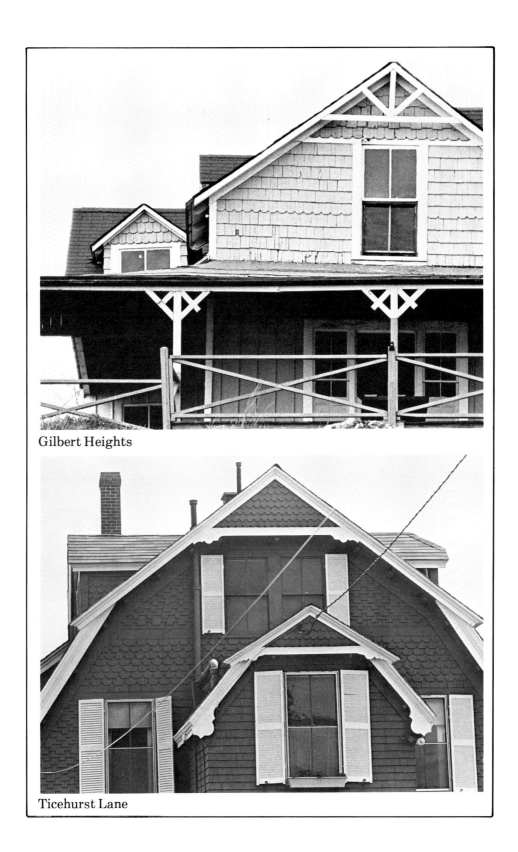

Gilbert Heights

Ticehurst Lane

40

The Queen Anne Style, 1880-1900

The original Queen Anne style referred to the period in England at the beginning of the 18th century at which time it was fashionable to mix Gothic and Renaissance motifs in architecture. Queen Anne Revival occurred in England during the late 1860's and was transported to America where it was popular from the later 1870's through the 1890's.

Queen Anne building was characterized by rich and varied exterior wooden decoration and strongly asymmetrical combinations of architectural forms including towers, projecting pavillions, porches, turrets, chimneys, and steep, multi-gabled roofs. A Palladian window (an arched window flanked by two shorter rectangular windows) on the facade was also a typical Queen Anne feature as was a rich mixture of textures, materials, and stained glass windows. The style often included wooden Eastlake decoration which was turned on a mechanical lathe and tended toward bulkiness (see description of Eastlake decoration). The Victorian Queen Anne building was painted in combinations of from three to five colors in order to delineate decorative details.

36 Pond Street

79 Pleasant Street

43

8 Devereux Street

8 Devereux Street

12-14 Watson Street

24 Waldron Street

70 Pleasant Street

Washington Square

18 Pearl Street

6 Devereux Street

78 Jersey Street

52

Eastlake Decoration, 1870-1900

Named after Charles Locke Eastlake (1833-1906), an English interior designer whose book *Hints on Household Taste* (1868) was very popular in the United States, Eastlake designs were originally intended for interior furnishings but were adapted in this country to architecture (much to Eastlake's horror).

Seeking inspiration from Gothic forms, Eastlake brackets, scrolls, perforated gables and pediments, bannisters and posts were turned on a mechanical lathe and today are recognizable by their bulkiness and Medieval influence.

Eastlake denounced all that he saw around him as vulgar and believed that if his 'basic principles' of design were followed, sturdy, simple (relatively speaking for the late Victorian period), and functional furnishings could be achieved. In the United States, Eastlake decoration was so popular that anything even slightly chunky, Medieval or geometric was touted as 'Eastlake;' eventually anything of improved taste was said to have been 'Eastlaked.'

Unusual for Marblehead, the house at 216 Pleasant Street, built in 1881, was decorated with considerable Eastlake detail which included an Oriental-inspired chrysanthemum/sunburst ornament on the tower.

Franklin Street

216 Pleasant Street

216 Pleasant Street

216 Pleasant Street

10 Guernsey Street

58

3 Maverick Street

5 Gerry Street

25 Devereux Street

60

The Shingle Style, 1880-1900

The Shingle Style house incorporated elements and motifs from the Romanesque, English Tudor, Colonial, and Gothic periods, and had ample space for the refined and comfortable life sought by well-to-do Americans at the end of the 19th century. The Shingle Style house was uniformly covered with unpainted wooden shingles, and was intended to harmonize with the landscape. It had a strong horizontal emphasis; frequently the interior space was extended to the outdoors through the use of verandas and porches. Gabled roofs with long, sloping sides and conical roofed towers were also typical features of the Shingle Style residence.

Although perhaps the most notable Shingle Style buildings were built in Newport, Rhode Island, the style was used in many fashionable suburban and vacation settings.

Robert Swain Peabody (1845-1917), partner in the firm of Peabody & Stearns, one of the oldest and best known architectural offices in Boston and among the favored firms in Newport, bought the Davis Road Shingle Style house on Peach's Point in 1887 and enlarged it to his taste over the years. He also built 'Castle Joyous,' the playhouse and studio next door, and several other Shingle Style residences in Marblehead.

257 Ocean Avenue

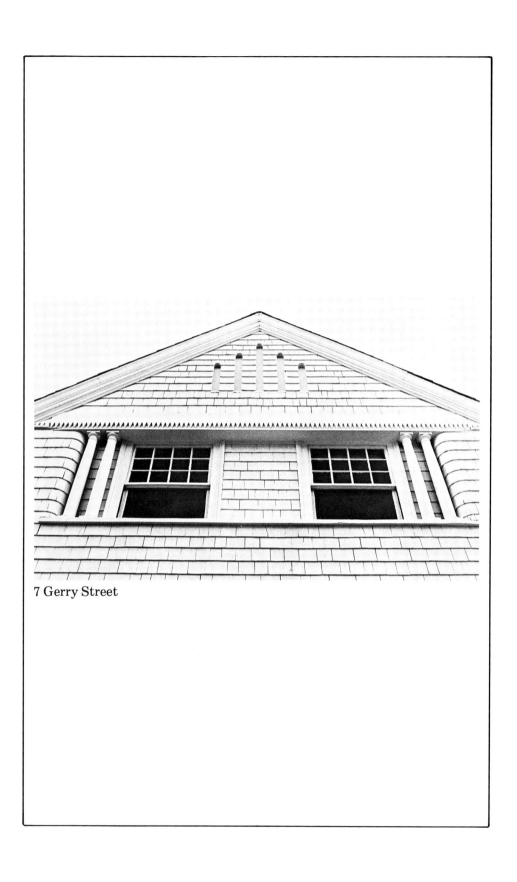

7 Gerry Street

7 Gerry Street

84 Harbor View

Corinthian Yacht Club, Marblehead Neck

Rockaway Avenue & Clifton Avenue

Davis Road

Davenport Road

60 Harbor Avenue

Cliff Street

Surf Street

70

The Victorian Gothic Style, 1860-1890

An outgrowth of the Gothic Revival Style (see description), the Victorian Gothic building also displayed steeply pitched roofs, irregular rooflines, asymmetrical organization, pointed arches, slate roofs, tall towers, turrets, and chimneys, but was distinguished from the earlier style primarily by a polychromatic exterior finish, particularly when it appeared in stone. Materials of different colors and textures, such as terra cotta tiles and carvings of foliage and animals, were used in addition to ornamental bricks which were commonly laid in goemetric patterns to decorate wall surfaces, arches, and doorways. Both pointed, arched, and straight-headed openings were employed in the Victorian Gothic building; in wood, the buildings were further characterized by heavier decoration than was seen in the Carpenter Gothic period and the absence of the vertical board and batten exterior wall treatment.

Dominating the Marblehead townscape much like a Gothic cathedral, Abbot Hall, the town hall of Marblehead, was designed by the Salem architectural firm of Lord & Fuller in 1876. Named after Benjamin Abbot, the benefactor who provided funds for its construction, Abbot Hall was designed to house an auditorium, library, storage vaults, and rooms for the use of town boards and offices. Still admired and treasured by Marblehead citizens, Abbot Hall is still in use as a town hall and has been declared a National Landmark.

Abbot Hall

73

Abbot Hall

View of Marblehead Harbor

74

18 Bessom Street

Abbot Hall

Abbot Hall

76

Abbot Hall

Abbot Hall

The Octagon House, 1850-1860

Octagonally shaped houses became a fad in the United States after the publication of a book by Orson Squire Fowler in 1848 entitled *A Home for All or the Gravel Wall and Octagon Mode of Building*. Fowler's book exerted a powerful influence upon the taste of the time and as a result by 1857 at least 1000 octagon houses were built in the United States. Fowler (1809-1887) was a phrenologist (evaluator of personality through interpretation of bumps on the head), lecturer, and writer on phrenology, health, self-culture, education and social reform. Fowler's 'invention' of the octagon house was largely a result of his phrenological activity, since he believed his prediliction toward building was revealed by his skull shape and qualified him to be an architect. Fowler's purpose was to provide a means 'to cheapen and improve human homes, and especially to bring comfortable dwellings within the reach of the poorer classes,' but because the octagon was expensive to build, the conveniences were found to be inconvenient, furniture arrangement was awkward, and the shape was considered 'poor in architectural appearance' since it did not blend with the landscape, the fad died out before the Civil War.

The octagon house on Mt. Vernon Street in Marblehead is one of three in Essex County. Built in 1865 by Thomas J. Bowden, a carpenter who owned a sawmill with his father on Sewall Street, the Marblehead octagon house was unusual in that originally all the rooms were square.

Octagon House, Abbot Street

Octagon House, Abbot Street

82

19th Century Commercial Brick Buildings in Marblehead, post 1888

After the fires of 1877 and 1888, the Town of Marblehead passed an ordinance which required that buildings over forty feet high be made of brick; several brick buildings in town therefore date from this period. Accustomed as they were to ornament on their wooden buildings, Victorian builders put considerable effort into the design, construction, and decoration of brick buildings. In Marblehead, details from Abbot Hall (1876) were imitated (albeit inexpensively) with the result that designs and patterns in brick and brick colors, arched windows and doorways, corbelling (stepped bricks), terra cotta cast decorations over doorways, and the carving of names and numbers in stone were common features of brick buildings in town.

The Rechabite Building was constructed in 1889 for the Rechabite Temperance Organization and was subsequently home to the Knights of Pythias who administered the building as a corporation until it was sold to a private party.

Pleasant & School Streets

18 Sewall Street

Pleasant Street

14 School Street

School Street (Central) Firehouse

School Street

90

The Alpine Chalet, 1840-1865, sporadic revivals thereafter

Because of its associations with the picturesque in Europe, the Alpine Chalet mode was chosen for sites reminiscent of the 'old country.' The influential Andrew Jackson Downing was especially partial to the Alpine Chalet mode for rocky mountainside locations since he believed that this variation of the Gothic Revival style was suitable to thick foliage and jagged terrain. Most characteristic of the Alpine Chalet style was the irregular roofline, terrace, stone foundation, two-color treatment of exterior surfaces, overhanging eaves, and sawn wood ornament, particularly the cut out bargeboards in the gable ends.

92

12 Gallison Avenue

94

The Chateau Style, 1860-1890, 1920's & 30's

Often inspired by a specific European model that either the owner or architect had seen abroad, the Chateau Style residence was massive, made of stone, irregular in silhouette, and incorporated many Renaissance features. It was distinguished by steeply pitched roofs, towers, turrets, and tall chimneys. Grand, formal and impressive, the Chateau Style was believed to be appropriate for the new American aristocracy that wished to emulate its European counterparts who lived in genuine chateaux. Because it required a large piece of land, the Chateau Style residence usually appeared in an expansive suburban setting.

'Carcassone,' a chateau in the French Norman Style, was designed by the architect Edgar Walker in 1934 for Mrs. Aroline C. Gove of Salem and her daughter Lydia Pinkham Gove, daughter and granddaughter of Lydia E. Pinkham of Vegetable Compound fame. Modeled after Carcassone Castle in France which the women had seen on a trip abroad, 'Carcassone' in Marblehead cost about half a million dollars to build. President Roosevelt commended the women for their dedication in building Carcassone because it employed so many people.

373 Ocean Avenue

98

The English Tudor Style, 1880-1914, 1920's & 30's

The original English Tudor period occurred during the 16th and first half of the 17th centuries, during which time the framework of buildings was left exposed and the spaces between were filled or 'nogged' and covered with plaster. Early English settlers brought this 'half-timbered' style to the Colonies and it was subsequently revived during the Victorian era as a facet of the 'picturesque.' The Tudor Revival Style was very popular in wealthy suburban settings around the turn of the century and until the First World War; it has been called 'Stockbroker's Tudor.'

The emphasis of the English Tudor Style was distinctly horizontal, cozy, and warm. A rustic appearance was achieved through the use of fine, natural materials amidst a natural setting. Other distinguishing features of this style were massive fireplaces, exposed beams, panelled wainscoting, and small, diamond-shaped panes in bay and oriel windows.

307 Ocean Avenue

Waldron Street

396 Ocean Avenue

102

341 Ocean Avenue

104

The Mission Style, 1890-1920

Although Spanish Colonial buildings appeared in the Southwestern United States in the 17th century and were viewed with interest from time to time throughout the 19th century, the Spanish Colonial building, or 'Mission' style residence, did not become fashionable in the East until the end of the 19th century. This phenomenon was partly due to increased travel abroad on the part of wealthy Americans who saw new architectural forms on the Continent, and partly to the European travel and training of American architects.

Characteristic of Mission style buildings of this latter period were rounded arches, stucco or plastered walls, a broad red-tiled roof which often extended beyond the walls, towers and balconies, projecting eaves, exposed rafters, asymmetrical massing, and irregularity of form.

246 Ocean Avenue was designed by Boston architect Frank Chouteau Brown (1876-1947) for Mrs. Isabella Stewart Gardner about 1910. Also called 'Twelve Lanterns,' the Spanish-inspired unique residence was commissioned by Mrs. Gardner for her protoge, George Proctor, a pianist.

246 Ocean Avenue

246 Ocean Avenue

108

The Colonial Revival Style 1880-1920

As a result of the 1876 Centennial Celebration, interest in American Colonial architecture was rekindled. Some Colonial Revival homes were accurate reproductions of earlier homes, but more frequently Colonial Revival houses were considerably larger than their Georgian predecessors and many of their parts were exaggerated or developed out of proportion to the rest of the building. The wooden trim on such houses was usually painted white against a pastel house body color. Other elements that were characteristic of Colonial Revival buildings were the columned portico, Palladian window, bow-front window, large brick chimney, and balconied entry portico or porch.

110

400 Ocean Avenue

400 Ocean Avenue

112

The American Castle, 1832-1914, 1920's & 30's

Whereas the true medieval castle in Europe was intended as a fortified residence capable of withstanding seige, the 19th century castle was a by-product of the Gothic Revival fascination with picturesque and romantic architecture.

Since they were 'picturesque' (as opposed to classical), castles built in the United States before the Civil War were at first considered architecturally avant garde and after Alexander Jackson Davis (1803-1892) designed Castle Glenellyn in 1832 for Robert Gilmore, a Baltimore merchant and art patron, the fashion for castellated mansions spread. By the end of the 19th century, however, the castle was considered a reactionary form that merely served nostalgic and eccentric needs. A few 19th century castles were built for scholarly and archaeological reasons, but castles from the latter part of the century were generally commissioned by rich Americans and industrial 'kings' who found that the castle form served as a vehicle for them to express their wealth, power, social position, and spurious aristocratic connections. A few castles, especially those of the 20th century, were ideosyncratic fantasies of their owners.

'Brahtalid,' meaning hewn out of rock in Icelandic, was built in Marblehead in 1927 by Waldo Ballard, an artist who also built, sold and renovated houses in Marblehead. It is alleged to be a replica of the 11th century Lief Ericson home in Greenland which Mrs. Ballard read about in a book. The castle was the residence of yacht designer L. F. Herreschoff between 1945 and his death in 1972.

114

Crocker Park Lane

Crocker Park Lane

115

116

The Neo Classical Revival Style, 1900-1920

The Neo Classical Revival style was frequently used in the design of public buildings such as courthouses, train stations, and post offices. Primarily based on motifs from the Greek orders (and occasionally from the Roman orders), features such as colossal columns, pedimented porticos, and parapets, were characteristically part of the monumental brick or stone Neo Classical Revival building.

The Old Main Post Office on Pleasant Street, the only example of the New Classical Revival style in Marblehead, was designed by the architectural firm of Peters & Rice in 1905. During the time of their collaboration, Arthur Wallace Rice (1869-1938) and William York Peters (1858-1930?) designed many distinctive Boston homes and suburban residences on the North Shore.

In addition to providing postal services, the Old Post Office was also the home of the Customs House Office between 1906 and 1929. In 1975 a new main Post Office opened on Smith Street in Marblehead, and although there was considerable interest in converting the Old Main Post Office for town purposes, in 1979 the building was sold to a private party.

118

Pleasant Street

Pleasant Street

120

The Triple Decker Style, 1890-1920

Modestly ornamented Triple Decker Style houses were common at the end of the 19th century and first quarter of the 20th century, especially in urban areas. Built by developers as moderate income housing for factory workers, the Triple Decker apartment offered pleasant accommodation and privacy for the tenant and was a good investment for the owner. There are numerous Triple Deckers in Chelsea, Dorchester, and Roxbury, but only one in Marblehead.

122

29 Pleasant Street

124

Details

60 Gregory Street

15 Sewall Street

128

216 Pleasant Street

57 Gregory Street

Harvard Street

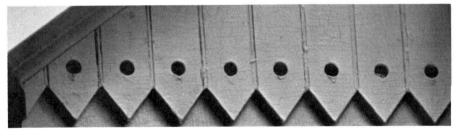

6 Phillips Street

130

8 Maverick Street

29 Pleasant Street

132

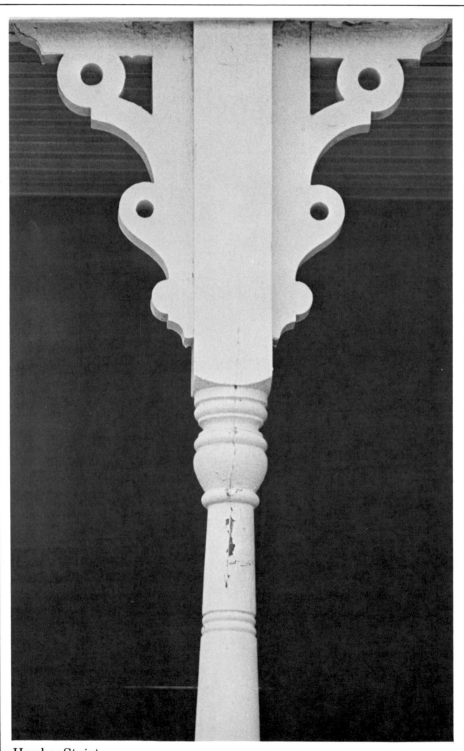

Hawkes Stréet

24 Maverick Street

133

8 Jefferson Street

72 Prospect Street

136

5 Bowden Street

16 Devereux Street

138

For Further Reading

Architecture, Ambition, and Americans by Wayne Andrews
New York: Harper and Bros., 1955.

Identifying American Architecture by John J.-G. Blumenson
Nashville: American Association for State and Local History, 1977.

American Building: The Historical Forces That Shaped It
by James Marston Fitch
New York: Schocken Books, 1973.

Old House Plans by Lawrence Grow
New York: Universe Books, 1978.

Architecture: Nineteenth and Twentieth Centuries
by Henry-Russell Hitchcock
Baltimore: Penguin Books, 1958.

American Buildings and Their Architects by William H. Jordy
New York: Anchor Books, 1976.

Carpenter Gothic by Alma deC. McArdle & Dierdre Bartlett McArdle
New York: Watson-Guptill Publications, 1978.

139

The Brown Decades: A Study of the Arts in America 1865-1895
by Lewis Mumford
New York: Dover Publications, 1971.

Sticks & Stones: A Study of American Architecture and Civilization
by Lewis Mumford
New York: Dover Publications, 1955.

Victorian Gardens: The Art of Beautifying Suburban Home Grounds
by Frank J. Scott
New York: Appleton & Co., 1870.

The Shingle Style by Vincent Scully
New Haven: Yale University Press, 1955.

American Architecture Since 1780: A Guide to the Styles
by Marcus Whiffen
Cambridge: MIT Press, 1969.

140

About the Authors

Gail Pike Hercher is an artist, teacher, historian and writer, with a special interest in late nineteenth and early twentieth century American art and architecture.

Michael Hercher, former Professor of Optics at the University of Rochester, New York, works as a laser physicist and does consulting in this field. He has worked as a photographer for the past 15 years.

The Herchers live in a Victorian house in Marblehead; this is their first book together.